A Reason For Buying Red Underwear

Poems about Life, Love & Other Stuff

by Jane Miles

Published by Jane Miles Publishing

© Jane Miles 2013

All rights reserved. No part of this publication may be reproduced, stored in a retrieval system, or transmitted in any form, or by any means, electronic, mechanical, photocopying, recording or otherwise, without the prior permission of Jane Miles.

Available by the same author:

'No Added Sugar'

(Poems succinctly reflecting segments of life, served with a light dusting of humour)

Print Production by

St Andrews Press
THE PRINTERS

www.standrewspress.co.uk

Contents

Reflections

A Reason For Buying Red Underwear	1
Secret Lover	2
Hair Today	3
Now and Then	4
Reality Check	5
Another Life	6
A Parting Gift	7
Love Is	8
Forgive and Forget	9
Lover's Lament	10
Anything You Can Do	11
Balance of Power	12
Dear John	13
Two Ears, One Mouth	14
Karma	15
Mirage	16
Forever Parallel	17
Chat Up	18
Division of Labour	19
Peppercorn	20
Him	21

Observations

In Praise of Maturity	25
A Vice By Any Other Name	26
The Power of Silence	27
Early Learning	28
The Age of Serenity	29
Naked Truth	30
When Silence is Golden	31
Speaking Out	32
Dare To Be Rare	33
Impostor	34
The Difference	35
A Word In Your Ear	36

Santa Lorena	37
From Experience	38
What Goes Around	39
Folklore	40
All You Need	41
None So Deaf	42

Wiseguy

Culture Shock	45
R.I.P. Sweetheart	46
Spiders and Flies	47
Happy Ever After	48
Last Tango In Brooklyn	49
Sweet Nothings	50
Something Like Passion	51
Things I Wish I Didn't Know (2)	52
His and Hers – A Moving Tale	53
Extras	54
He Said, She Said	55
What It Means	56
Cheapskate	57
Location, Location, Location	58
Paper Hero	59
Brooklyn Casanova	60
For The Record	61
Absolution Denied	62
Cetera Desunt	63
One Of Us	64
An Absence of Logic	65
War Game	66
The Essential Difference	67
Loser	68
Parting Shot	69
The Project	70

Just a Number

Rewind	73
Stage Fright	74
Age of Consent	75

Ode To A Tart	76
Pudding Club	77
Sex and Chocolate	78
A Passing Thought	79
Primadonna	80
No Place To Hide	81
Heaven and Hell	82
Body Image	83
Last Gasp	84
Tits Up	85
The Big 'O'	86
The Mistress	87
Instant Mash	88

To Be Serious for a Moment

Helpless	91
With The Benefit of Hindsight	92
Night Shift	93
Wasted	94
Thanks For Nothing	95
Twisted	96
Payback	97

A Bit Of A Rant

To My Critics	101
Busy	102
Gone	103
Burning Ambition	104
In Praise of Artists	105
Different Strokes	106
Junkie	107
Too Little, Too Late	108
Techno-Curse	109
Aesthetic Pause	110
Art and Soul	111
Appetiser	112
Skin Deep	113
Little Gods	114
One Man's Meat	115
Censorship: The New Chaos?	116

Acknowledgements

Thank you to Sandy, my miracle-working hairdresser, whose single-word question: "Well?" every time I walked into her salon, has finally shamed me into getting this book assembled, organised and printed.

And to Tiff for her unwavering encouragement and for saying "go for it" at just the right moment!

To Jason and Alex for allowing me to display my first book in their restaurant, and to Beth, Emma and Lydia for feedback.

To Frank and Luciano for having 'No Added Sugar' on the window ledge, next to *The Telegraph* and the *Wells Journal*, in Bar Italia.

And lastly, thanks to Richie, full-time scumbag, for being reliably exasperating and therefore the perfect muse.

"Those who know they are profound strive for clarity. Those who would like to seem profound strive for obscurity."

Friedrich Nietzsche

Reflections

A Reason for Buying Red Underwear

Heaven knows, it wasn't much,
It wasn't love, or ... not as such.
I suppose you could call it a 'part-time affaire',
Or a reason for buying red underwear.

Secret Lover

I have a secret lover
Who belongs to another.

I love the way he talks
And moves and walks.

To me his presence is essential,
His status (marital) inconsequential.

And late at night his body is all mine
As is his cheating and his lying.

But for now I'll take the smooth with the rough,
Until I've had enough.

Hair Today

It's not that I'm shallow or unkind,
That I want your body and not your mind,
But whoever cut your hair that style
Was a cruel, untalented Delilah.

I know what counts is what's inside,
And I should have been tactful, I could have lied.
I could have said: Hey, your hair looks great!
I could have, but didn't, and now it's too late.

Now and Then

How I miss my Prince
Of Darkness. No-one since
Has made me laugh,
Or had half
His sex-appeal,
Or made me feel
This good, and bad.
Somehow it's sad
That we just let it go,
And I don't know
If we'll ever meet again.
Now and then
I think of him,
And every minute in
Between. Perhaps sometimes he
Thinks of me.

Reality Check

He purred: "Can I move in with you?
I need you and love you to bits."
But what he really wanted was
Central-heating, Sky TV,
And a housekeeper with big tits.

Another Life

In another life I'm happy, bright, intelligent and strong,
But when you're near it all goes wrong.

I lose my appetite, my reason and control;
For you I'd even sell my soul.

In another life I'm quite assertive, and I'm clever;
Then you don't phone and I'm weak as ever.

You're so selfish, mean and mentally abusive,
And when I need you, uncannily elusive.

Is there any medication, any cure –
So I won't need you any more?

Or am I doomed to be for evermore afflicted,
Constrained and addicted?

No. For in my other world I'm coping and I'm fine
And can at least pretend you're mine.

A Parting Gift

A word in your ear, my Sweet,
Before you go:

Try to turn up sober, if you can;
Remove the chewing-gum before you kiss;
Never wear your socks and pants in bed,
Or call her by your wife's name (enough said).

And remember:

The hand-job can wait until you've said Hello,
And tits are made of flesh, not pizza dough.

And before you assume
That her little world revolves around you,
Remember W.H.O.T. – that's right –
Women Have Orgasms Too.

So off you go my Pet,
"Ciao" and "Take Care",
But next time
Grate your Parmesan elsewhere.

Love Is

An emotional guillotine, and
Losing control;
Eternal compromise, and
Selling your soul.

Forgive and Forget

Forgiving's not the problem,
Don't you see?
You're just not the man
I needed you to be.

Lover's Lament

Please! Spare me
All the tired and worn excuses.
It seems to me
That you're as married
As it suits you to be,
And as busy as it takes
Not to be free.

Anything You Can Do

If you need to play mind-games,
That's fine by me;
I'll play meaner and dirtier
Than you, as you'll see.

Balance of Power

Don't let me tell you how to be
Or be too sweet and 'there for me';
Don't let me tell you even this,
Don't give me the chance –
Just give me a kiss . . .

Dear John

I would rather take poison, my Angel,
Than come back to you again;
Or pull out my finger nails, one by one,
Or fry to death under desert sun:
Any of these would be more fun
Than to be with you again.

Two Ears, One Mouth

The basic difference
Between us, my Dear,
Is that I try to listen,
While you merely hear.

Karma

You sated all your appetites,
Indulged in every mortal sin;
Now your 'circulatory problem' means
You can neither get it up, nor in.

Mirage

I fell in love with what might have been –
His potential was all I could see;
And when the reality didn't fit,
There was no-one around to blame, but me.

Forever Parallel

He loves me in his way, I
Love him in mine –
Shame the two
Don't coincide.

Chat up

'How do you like to wake up?' he asked,
'With tea, coffee, or me?'
As propositions go, I thought,
I've heard better, and worse,
So we'll see . . .

Division of Labour

We have a great system, my man and I –
We split the chores fairly, which entails
That I pen the occasional poem,
And he does everything else.

Peppercorn

Antonio! That's some pepper mill –
Does it grind as well as twist?
I've seen a few around Bristol,
But this must be one I've missed;
So smooth and brown, yet . . . functional,
'Almost phallic', to coin a phrase.
Would you sprinkle a little more please,
On my spaghetti bolognese?

Of course, Signora, at Sergio's
We always aim to please . . .
Is there anything else I can serve you with?
Would you like some Parmesan cheese?
As long as it's fresh, I'll have some,
Will you grate it at the table?
I'll grate it wherever you wish, Signora,
And as freshly as I'm able.

Did you enjoy your meal, Signora?
Can I get you anything more?
A cappuccino, or espresso?
Oh really? Well, if you're sure
There's nothing else I can tempt you with,
From the menu, anyway . . .
Arrivederci, until tomorrow then,
And be sure to have a nice day . . .

Him

It's over, it's finished, he's gone;
He fucked up once too often.

For a while from his arse the sun shone,
Then went in and was lost and forgotten.

Observations

In Praise of Maturity

Do you really think
That just because some parts
Of us are sagging,
That for every piece of
Younger ass we're gagging?
Or that your ability to
Get it up more often and for longer
Makes you more desirable?
Oh please – we women
Of a certain age are stronger
And more choosey than you know.
We've made a few trips
Round the block, and so
Are not impressed with
Youth for youth's sake,
And would rather be alone
Than settle for a lager
And testosterone.

A Vice By Any Other Name

Honesty: a much venerated virtue
Which, from the mouths of some,
Aims, hits, and effectively annihilates.

The Power of Silence

The words we say, once heard,
Can be regretted, retracted,
Disavowed, or even denied;
They can never be unsaid.

Early Learning

"Don't put it in your mouth, Dear,
Unless you know where it's been", she'd say.
It was good advice sixty years ago,
And is just as relevant today.

The Age Of Serenity

Is being still young enough
To enjoy it,
But old enough
Not to need it.

Naked Truth

The mark of a Man has always been
The part of him that's never seen.
Not even when completely nude
Will you catch a glimpse of his attitude.

When Silence Is Golden

The world is full of men
Confessing to women
Who'd rather not know.

Speaking Out

For the preservation of Liberty
I would lose my own –
For this, and for this alone.

Dare To Be Rare

If an object's rarity increases its value,
Why do so many strive for
A level of physical perfection
That reduces them to bland uniformity?

Impostor

Beware of Need
Masquerading as Love –
The vulture
Dressed as a dove.

The Difference

You'll rarely hear
A woman say,
'It was only sex',
And expect to be forgiven.

A Word In Your Ear

Worth knowing, as
You leave her bed, is
That women and elephants
Never forget.

Santa Lorena

How many of us long to,
But will never have the guts
To creep in while he's sleeping
And make the cruellest cut.

From Experience

Some are born good lovers,
Some learn along the way,
Some need the stars to find the zones,
And some have to go without, or pay.

What Goes Around

Pay attention all you predatory women –
Your modus operandi at the very least
Lacks class, and will before too long
Return to bite you in the arse.

Folklore

If you want to keep him
In your bed,
Make him laugh and
Give good head.

All You Need

So much has been written
About love,
Which, however good,
Is never enough.

None So Deaf

They never listen, do they –
Just hear what they want to hear,
Then wallow in self-pity
And whine that nobody cares.

wiseguy

Culture Shock

"Men are from Mars",
Or so says John Gray;
Some are from even further away:
Some are from Brooklyn, U.S. of A.

R.I.P. Sweetheart

Should anything awful happen to you,
I'd try to stay dignified and brave;
And I'd try not to step on the flowers, my Love,
While dancing, nightly, on your grave.

Spiders and Flies

With habitual liars
You know the score:
When they say "The sky's blue",
You look up to make sure.

"I tell the truth some of
The time", he'd say,
But even stopped clocks
Can be right twice a day.

Happy Ever After

Even after everything you've done,
We're still together, side by side:
How else could I stay close enough
To lace your beer with cyanide?

Last Tango in Brooklyn

You just 'danced' with her – oh, really?
Is that what they call it these days?
Do your two left feet match her dainty size nines
Every time the orchestra plays?

Sweet Nothings

What do you mean I'm breaking your heart –
How could I break what doesn't exist?
Your ego, on the other hand,
Could be half the size, and hard to miss.

Something Like Passion

As long as you're in the world, I have to have you;
As long as your heart is beating, we two are one;
As long as you're drawing breath, my equilibrium is cursed;
As long as you live, I'll find no peace under the sun.

Things I Wish I Didn't Know (2)

That you Look and Want a
Hundred times a day, but
Never Touch, or at least
That's what you always say.

His and Hers – A Moving Tale

I just can't seem to get my head
Around an ex, a van, and a bed.
The ex is his, the bed as well,
But never 'combined', or so he tells
Me. The van is hers, and I guess must be
The only one left in NYC.

The offer, of course, was hers – how kind,
And how lucky for him that he managed to find
Such a generous creature, with tits and a van,
And how lucky am I to know such a man.

Extras

Her manoeuvring skills must be truly amazing;
Linguistic agility, something mean;
Or why would you part with a thousand dollars
For 'legal services', sight unseen?

He Said, She Said

Are you saying I can't have female friends?
It IS only friendship, not sex.

I'm saying I'd feel a lot happier
If this 'friend' of yours weren't an 'ex'.

But that was all over years ago,
There's nothing between us now.

If you say so, Dear, but I wonder –
Have you told the Sacred Cow?

What It Means

Don't say, "I didn't mean to hurt you", say
"I didn't give you a second's thought",
And don't say, "I'm really, truly sorry", say
"I'm truly sorry that I got caught".

Cheapskate

Don't try to convince me;
Talk is cheap:
You're only as good
As the promises you keep.

Location, Location, Location

You'd like me to burn in Hell, I know,
Or wait a few eons in Purgatory:
Having spent three years with you, my Love,
It would feel exactly like home, to me.

Paper Hero

You say you'd take
A bullet for me,
Safe in the knowledge that
Such a noble sacrifice
Would never be required.

Brooklyn Casanova

All the women there were,
And the liar you are –
Just one Linda too many,
And a Donna too far.

For The Record

If you'd kept the story simple –
Not tried to be too clever:
If you'd been a better liar
We might still be together.

Absolution Denied

Don't tell me again how sorry you are –
No more facile whimperings after the fact;
Try exercising some foresight, Dear –
Try not committing the act.

Cetera Desunt

A promise intended
To pacify
Is no more, or less
Than a split-level lie.

One Of Us

"The only way
We'll be separated now
Is if one of us dies", he said.

I know him too well
To assume 'by natural causes',
And myself not well enough
To know which one.

An Absence of Logic

So many articulate reasons why
I should have walked away;
Just one incoherent need
Compelling me to stay.

War Game

That friend of yours
Is a waste of space;
He saved your life,
I rest my case.

The Essential Difference

Is our definition of the
Verb 'to cheat': to trick or
Deceive; to be unfaithful,
Especially sexually.

We firmly believe that the
Oral Experience fits quite
Neatly into that description, and
That whether or not you kiss them
Is irrelevant.

Your attempts to enter into
A debate on the subject –
Interestingly, after the fact –
Cut no ice, and are
Of little interest.

Loser

As you lie in your deep, dark pool of self-pity,
Your self-inflicted abyss,
Pause for a moment, Richard,
Pause, and ask yourself this:
"Did this sorry state just happen to me,
  An unlucky quirk of fate?
  Am I the innocent victim here,
  Or the serial perpetrator?"
And don't think of yourself as misunderstood –
We understand you only too well,
Your father, ex-wife, ex-girlfriend and I,
And the judges who sent you to jail.
We've all rumbled you, my Petal,
So there's no use stamping and crying:
And before you even open your mouth,
We also know when you're lying.

Parting Shot

You're free to wreck your own life
If that's what you feel compelled to do,
But I can't and won't allow you
To wreak your havoc on my life too.

The Project

He had kerb appeal
And huge potential,
But after seven years
Cracks appeared in
His supporting walls,
So I handed back the keys.

Just A Number

Rewind

They tell me, 'It's only a number',
'It comes to us all', 'You're as young as you feel',
But I'll handle it in my own way, thanks –
Kicking and screaming, in total denial.

Stage Fright

The mirrors are covered,
The lights turned down –
A few vampires having fun?
Well, actually, no –
Just the setting for
Some sex at sixty-one.

Age of Consent

The government's handing me money,
My prescriptions are free – that's great,
But the drivers knowing how old I am?
No way – the bus-pass can wait.

Ode to a Tart

I've just eaten Bitter Chocolate Torte
When I knew I ought not to be greedy,
But emotionally I'm needy.

I can't resist temptation, and I'm weak;
So sue me – I'm a woman not a freak.

When it comes to being 'strong'
I can't be arsed;
Give me chocolate, sex and Pleasure
First and last.

Others worship cars, and some religion;
I made a different decision.

Pudding Club

I shouldn't, but . . . oh what the hell;
And I'll have a bite of yours as well.
Yes, of course I can justify it –
Just give me time . . . and one more bite.

Sex and Chocolate

Sex and chocolate can be enjoyed
In very similar ways:
Quality over Quantity,
And a rest every three days.

A Passing Thought

Love is beautiful,
Sex sublime:
So many men,
So little time . . .

Primadonna

Exit stage left
Inadequate lover.
Run along home
And cry to your mother.
I'm back centre stage,
My audience awaits:
She is lost, so they say,
Who hesitates.

No Place To Hide

Never, ever wear leather trousers –
They'll just emphasise what you're trying to hide.
If someone told you they suited you,
They shouldn't have; they lied.

Sex appeal isn't something you wear, like a hat –
It's something you're born with, or not:
And if not, leather trousers won't change that –
They'll never give what you haven't got.

Heaven and Hell

Heaven is safe and nice, no spice
But Hell is where I run, more fun.

Heaven is tranquil and good, but that's
Not me. I'm off to Hell and Häagan Dazs.

Body Image

He says he likes me as I really am,
But I don't know –
Is he just being kind, or blind?

Can he really want to stroke my cellulite?
Might that be unrealistic, or fantastic?
Could he be more desperate than enthusiastic?

I wish that I could see me through his eyes,
But I despise this heap of blubber that is me.

So we'll make out in light that's very dim,
And I'll pretend that I am loved by him
And not with every sigh be asking, Why?

Last Gasp

"Should I grow old gracefully now, d'you think?
Let it go grey, with a sensible cut?"
"Not while you're still breathing", my stylist replies,
So 'elderly babe' it is then, or not.

Tits Up

How I hate the ones
That lift and separate.
Mine point south-east and -west,
So what's best
For them are ones that
Push together and up,
In a 38C cup.

'Cos tits that look
Like spaniels' ears
Attract no whistles,
Only sneers.

So something brief and racey,
Satin and lacey;
I'll knock 'em dead
In black and red.
Men never want to have a fling
With girls in cotton scaffolding.

The Big 'O'

When pursued or rushed
Can become extinct:
Often faked, originals
Much rarer than you think.

The Mistress

There she sits. Same table, same time.
Arrives at eight, still waiting at nine.
Does she really believe that he'll leave his wife?
Perhaps he will, in another life.

Instant Mash

Blow out the candles
Switch off the heat –
I don't need to see
And I don't want to eat –
Foreplay, three-play, two-play
Who cares?
Come over here –
And show me who dares . . .

To Be Serious For A Moment

Helpless

You're slipping away
And there's nothing I can do;
Slipping away
And I can't help you,
Or turn back time.

You're slipping away
And leaving me. Don't go –
Slipping away
And I don't know
If I can bear it.

With the Benefit of Hindsight

Only after they died
Did I realise
That my parents were people
Before I arrived.

Night Shift

The TV's off and all is quiet
In the middle of the night
While I write.

In the daylight hours there are distractions
No opportunity or time
For rhyme.

The days provide ideas and inspiration
That tends to be their role,
Food for the soul.

Some nights I simply go to bed
Because although my soul is fed
My brain is dead.

Wasted

I'm not angry anymore, just
Sad and disappointed that
You didn't love enough, but at
The same time, loved too much.

Thanks For Nothing

I cry for what we
Could have been, and
Should have been but,
Thanks to you, never
Would have been.

Twisted

Your lies make me a person
I don't like, or even know –
Part teacher, part cop, part therapist.
I wish it were otherwise,
But those lies knock the ground
From beneath my feet, tie knots
In my soul, what's left of it.

Payback

For lying to me
The price you pay
Is I'll never believe
Another word you say.

A Bit of a Rant

To My Critics

I don't pretend that what
I write's Great Art;
I just write it as I see it
And that's a start.

Critics will judge me and their praise
May well be sparse,
But I won't hear them from where I'm hiding,
Up my own creative arse.

Busy

Always 'busy, busy, busy',
Never there when you phone,
Never home.
Always rushing here and there, and everywhere.

No time to simply Be,
Or really See.
Always rushing past, too fast.

Up at dawn and always Doing,
Or Pursuing, High Achieving.
Never staying, always leaving.

OK, all right, so let them be,
But keep them well away from me.
I'm not impressed,
Or even dressed.

Gone

Let me be gone
When the pen's obsolete,
When only screens chat
And people don't meet.

Burning Ambition

If I spend my future creating a Past,
Live every day as if it's my last,
Transgress and give in to every temptation,
Will I qualify for Hell and damnation?
I mean Heaven's O.K., but for pity's sake,
Just how much 'goodness' can one person take?

In praise of Artists

Artists, writers and poets
Have always understood
The human psyche better
Than scientists ever could.

Different Strokes

I've never been a romantic soul,
I'm well aware of the fact.
I've always believed that humour
Is the ultimate aphrodisiac.

Junkie

Someone in my life once said
'Addiction' is whatever you rely on
When you're under stress, whatever
Fed your need, what you get by on.

So by that token one could say
I'm just a hopeless case by definition,
With no cure in sight, but hey –
I'll see some action, rather than just wishing.

Too Little, Too Late

"I'm sorry", doesn't reach the spot,
"I'm sorry", doesn't change a lot,
"I'm sorry", doesn't make it good,
However much I wish it could.

Techno-Curse

A curse on all computers
Or, better yet
A deadly virus on the Net.

They're a vice like any other,
And I think you'll find
That carried to excess
They'll make you blind.

Aesthetic Pause

The triumph of self-belief over talent, I fear,
Is the sole source of many a celebrity career.
And economy over quality will, in the end,
To the depths of artistic oblivion surely descend.

And after one too many estuary inflections,
These days my recreational direction
Lies where what isn't worth saying or hearing's
   left unsaid,
And where genius transcends the unmade bed.

Art and Soul

Great Art is what it is
Because it survives the test of time;
It transcends the merely pretty
To reach beyond, to the ultimate Sublime.

Appetiser

Before you think about lying to me,
Make sure you have a good memory,
Because liars are my speciality –
I eat them for breakfast, dinner and tea.

Skin Deep

One day I think I'd like to be
The me I really need to be;
The me I hope I've always been,
Concealed beneath a different skin.

Little Gods

Little gods whose role it is to cure our ills,
Little gods with no communication skills,

Little gods defended by the GMC
Can maim, abuse, and kill, and still go free.

Little gods released into communities
Are faced with many tempting opportunities.

The notes will never read: "Abused Miss B today",
And she will keep the secret, it's the easier way.

But little gods in ivory towers have often found
That little worms eventually can turn around.

One Man's Meat

Don't impose your truth on me,
Your good and bad,
Your right and wrong,
Your black and white,
Your weak and strong.
That works for you,
But not for me:
I choose to sing a different song.

Censorship: the New Chaos?

If we can go to jail for
What we see, and think about,
Who judges those who judge us,
About who goes 'in', and who stays 'out'?

And how long before the Dream Police,
Or the Mood Police, or worse?
Exaggerate? I hope so,
But many a true word has been spoken in verse.